Energy And Action
WORKING MACHINES

John Marshall, Ed.D.

The Rourke Book Co., Inc.
Vero Beach, Florida 32964

PHOTO CREDITS
All photos © J.M. Patten

Library of Congress Cataloging-in-Publication Data

Marshall, John, 1944-
    Working machines / John Marshall.
        p. cm. — (Energy and action)
    Includes index.
    Summary: Describes simple machines and how they work, including
the inclined plane, levers, wheels and axles, the wedge, screws, and
pulleys.
    ISBN 1-55916-155-8
    1. Machinery—Juvenile literature. [1. Machinery. 2. Simple
machines.] I. Title. II. Series.
TJ147.M32 1995
621.8—dc20   95-16003
                                        CIP
                                        AC

Printed in the USA

TABLE OF CONTENTS

TERRIFIC MACHINES

Machines are terrific inventions!

Let's read all about **simple machines** (SIM puhl muh SHEENZ) and discover how they make work easier to do.

Long ago, people discovered that they were not strong enough to do some jobs. Using just their bodies to move logs or lift heavy rocks was too hard.

Just like you, these people used good thinking to solve problems. They invented machines to help them do work. These machines helped them chop wood, carry heavy loads and dig holes.

An "old" scientist thinks about machines.

SIMPLE MACHINES

Today we call these first machines *simple machines*. They only have a few moving parts— or even none at all. Simple machines changed how people lived long ago.

You may be surprised to find out that you use simple machines every day. You may even have a few right in your bedroom.

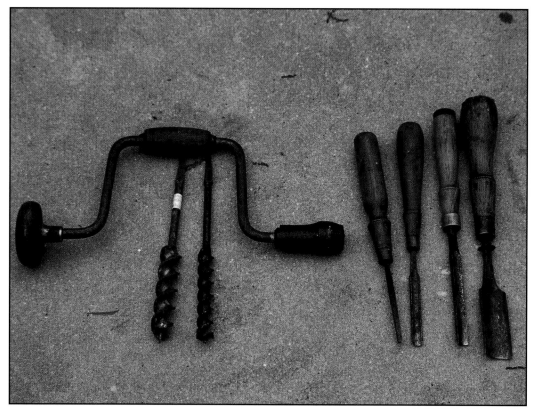

Drill bits and wedges are examples of simple machines.

Wheels and axles, and levers are parts of a complex lawn mower.

All machines, simple or not, have one thing in common—they help do work.

Inventors, people who make new things, put simple machines together to make bigger ones, like automobiles. Maybe the inventor in you will be able to use simple machines to put together—a homework machine!

INCLINED PLANES

Simple machines can change the amount of force you need to do work. With a machine you don't need to push or pull as hard.

An **inclined plane** (in KLYND PLAYN) is not an airplane. It is a simple machine that makes it easier to move an object to a higher or lower place.

Inclined means slanted, and a plane is a flat surface. Inclined planes are flat surfaces that slant. Bike and wheelchair ramps are inclined planes.

A playground slide is an inclined plane.
It's flat and slanted.

LET'S MOVE A REFRIGERATOR!

Making an inclined plane is as simple as placing a board on a slant to make a ramp.

Lifting a refrigerator into a truck sounds like an impossible job. It is just too heavy to lift straight up.

However, a strong person could push a refrigerator up your ramp, an inclined plane, and into the truck.

Pushing the refrigerator all the way up the ramp is a longer distance than lifting it straight up, but it takes less force to move the refrigerator along.

This inclined plane makes moving day much easier.

MOVE IT WITH A LEVER!

You found the perfect spot to put up the tent—except for that rock in the middle of the campground. The rock is big and heavy, but you can move it with a simple machine call a **lever** (LEHV er).

A lever is a bar or board used for lifting or moving an object. The longer the bar or board, the easier the work is to do.

This scale is a kind of lever. The weight on one side forces the other side up.

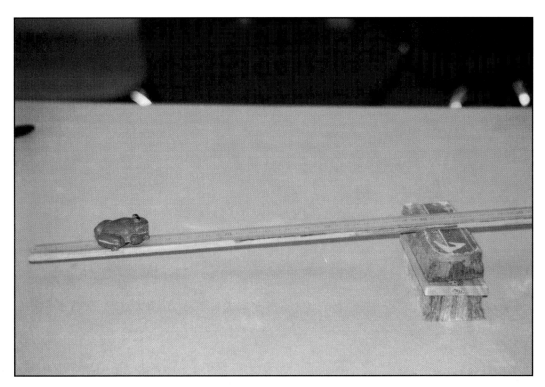

An eraser is the fulcrum, or resting spot, on this clever lever.

Let's use a lever to move that pesky rock away. Push one end of your board under the side of the rock. Place a log under the board near the rock. The log is called a **fulcrum** (FUL krum), the place where the lever will rest.

Push down on the high end of the board. The board, pivoting or turning on your log fulcrum, will move the rock out of the middle of your campsite.

WHEELS AND AXLES IN YOUR ROOM!

You probably have a doorknob on your bedroom door. Guess what? A doorknob is a simple machine called a **wheel and axle** (WEEL AND AKS el).

A wheel and axle is made of a wheel attached to a post, or rod, called an axle. By turning the wheel, the axle turns, too. This movement helps do work.

Turning a doorknob, which is a kind of wheel, turns an axle inside the door. This makes the door unlatch and latch, so you can open or close it.

Here's a simple machine you probably have right in your bedroom!

SPLIT IT WITH A WEDGE

Ouch! The sewing needle pricks your finger as you sew on a button. When you use knives, axes, scissors and nails you need to be very careful and have an adult help you.

All these objects are sharp. They can poke holes, and cut and split things. Each is a simple machine called a **wedge** (WEJ).

Wedges have a special shape that helps to do work. An ax has a thin, sharp end that makes the first cut into a piece of wood. The other end is thicker and is good for splitting the wood apart.

A hatchet is a wedge used for chopping.
Careful, it's sharp!

SCREWS HOLD TIGHT!

We think of **screws** (SKROOZ) and nails as being pretty much alike. They hold things together. However, a screw is a different kind of simple machine.

Screws have a ridge called a **thread** (THRED) that winds evenly around it, from top to bottom. A groove on top lets you put in a screwdriver to turn the screw.

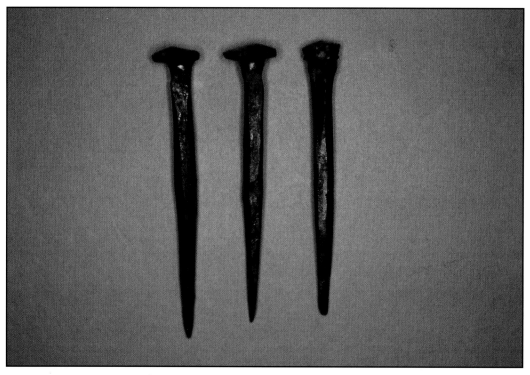

Nails are wedges used to hold things together.

Pounding a nail is faster than turning a screw.

It takes a longer time to turn a screw than to pound the same size nail into a board. Let's see why.

Imagine unwinding the thread from the screw. You would see it is much longer than a straight nail. Moving all that thread into the board takes longer to do, but it really holds things tightly together.

PULLEYS HELP RAISE FLAGS

Raising the flag at school is an important job. You or the custodian pull down on the rope and the flag goes up the flagpole.

At the top of the pole is a simple machine called a **pulley** (PUL ee). A pulley is a small wheel with a groove around it to hold a rope. Pull on the rope and this wheel turns round and round like a bicycle wheel.

Pulleys are used to move heavy things, too. The grooved wheel turns easily when the rope is pulled. This means less force is needed to move the object and get the work done.

Pulleys do work by lifting loads that are heavy, or too far away to reach.

GLOSSARY

fulcrum (FUL krum) — resting spot for a lever

inclined plane (in KLYND PLAYN) — a slanted, flat surface

lever (LEHV er) — a board or bar supported on a fulcrum, used for lifting

pulley (PUL ee) — a grooved wheel and rope

screw (SKROO) — a thread wrapped around a post

simple machine (SIM puhl muh SHEEN) — a machine with few or no moving parts

thread (THRED) — a ridge that winds evenly around a screw

wedge (WEJ) — a simple machine that starts out thick at one end and gets thin at the other edge

wheel and axle (WEEL AND AKS el) — a wheel attached to a post

A crank is a kind of wheel. This simple machine is a wheel and axle.

INDEX